Reader's Guides

SECOND SERIES 9

THE HISTORY OF FLYING

by

CHARLES H. GIBBS-SMITH

T0345968

PUBLISHED FOR

THE NATIONAL BOOK LEAGUE

AT THE UNIVERSITY PRESS

CAMBRIDGE

1957

CAMBRIDGE UNIVERSITY PRESS
Cambridge, New York, Melbourne, Madrid, Cape Town,
Singapore, São Paulo, Delhi, Mexico City

Cambridge University Press
The Edinburgh Building, Cambridge CB2 8RU, UK

Published in the United States of America by Cambridge University Press, New York

www.cambridge.org
Information on this title: www.cambridge.org/9781107622203

First published 1957
Re-issued 2013

A catalogue record for this publication is available from the British Library

ISBN 978-1-107-62220-3 Paperback

CONTENTS

INTRODUCTION

It is natural, in a nation surrounded by water, that the maritime traditions are so easily and enthusiastically preserved and transmitted from generation to generation; and natural, too, that the history of coaches, carriages and railways—and now automobiles—should find enthusiasts in a land that did so much to make such machines reliable and popular. By the same token one might have supposed that when Englishmen first took to the air in the eighteenth century, such a revolutionary and romantic departure from conventional locomotion might have made its mark, and laid down a firm tradition of its own, to be deepened by the adventure and glory that followed through the years. For adventure, discovery and heroism were to accompany airborne vehicles as they transported men and women on novel explorations of land and sky; and when aircraft were pressed into the service of war, the deeds performed within their frail structures matched any that were done on land or sea. But no true tradition of the air, comparable with that attached to other means of locomotion, has been created—unless it be the rather more narrow and military tradition of the Royal Flying Corps and Royal Air Force dating from the year 1912. One day I hope we shall see the myths and the legends and the events of aerostation and aviation growing into a strong dramatic tributary of history; shall feel the tradition flourishing and taking hold. In this process, the continuous stream of books which has been appearing since the later years of the eighteenth century will play an important part and lend substance to the subject. Perhaps it will come as a surprise to some readers to discover how rich and

5

varied is the literary field of flying, and what a delightful field it is.

The first full-dress textbook on flying in the English language was published before the French Revolution, in the year 1785. It was by Tiberius Cavallo (an Italian domiciled here) and called *The History and Practice of Aerostation*, the latter word referring to lighter-than-air flight. The balloon had been invented in 1783 and this was the first serious treatise on the subject to appear in Britain.

The nineteenth century fairly bristled with books on flying; books good, bad and indifferent. There were the crackpots—always with us—who had their say; the scientists—mostly after 1850; the men of action who flew balloons and experimented with gliders; and the story-tellers.

But concerning the greatest 'airman' of the century there is little to be sought and found by the book collector or even the reader; for Sir George Cayley, who is the world's true father of scientific aeronautics, published his work in three rare series of periodical issues—Nicholson's *Journal of Philosophy* (1809–10), Tilloch's *Philosophical Magazine* (1816–17), and the *Mechanics Magazine* (1837).

But in other fields there is good and delightful hunting. One of the most rewarding Victorian works on the air is C. Hatton Turner's *Astra Castra* (1865), a huge pot-pourri of good and bad accounts of aerial efforts of all ages. Despite its poorly reproduced illustrations—one of them is mis-titled into the bargain—it is a classic, and should be in every air-minded library.

More specialised treasures to look for are—to go back again—V. Lunardi's *Account of the First Aerial Voyage in England* (1784), and T. Monck Mason's *Aeronautica* (1838). The first speaks for itself, and the second is an able account of the great Victorian long distance record of the air, when Mason with the pilot Charles Green and Robert Hollond

6

flew non-stop from London to Weilburg in the German Duchy of Nassau in 1836; a remarkable flight of some 480 miles.

Also still obtainable by the sharp-eyed is J. Glaisher's *Travels in the Air* (1870) translated from the French and containing not only some thrilling stories of ballooning but many fine wood engravings and some coloured lithographs.

Another translation from the French is W. de Fonvielle's *Adventures in the Air* (1877), a 'must' for aerial book lovers, which contains a dramatic series of (mostly true) adventures.

The balloon pilots themselves sometimes wrote their reminiscences, and H. T. Coxwell's *My Life and Balloon Experiences* (2 vols., 1887–89) is well worth the few shillings you will probably be asked for it.

Balloon enthusiasts should also consult the great published collections of aeronautical illustrations by Bruel, Grand-Carteret, Dollfus, Lockwood-Marsh, and Hodgson— those in Dollfus and Hodgson being ancillary to voluminous and accurate text material—and the now rare catalogues issued by Messrs. Maggs.

For the collector, one of the great nineteenth-century 'catches' is a book not on balloons but on heavier-than-air machines, which still turns up once in a while: it is an American work, Octave Chanute's *Progress in Flying Machines* (1894) which is not only a great rarity, but the most valuable mine of information about heavier-than-air experiments to that date.

Please do not deride, still less pass by for their historical importance, the translations of Jules Verne's famous romances of the last century, especially his *Clipper of the Clouds*. He was a remarkable man, with great vision and a powerful ability to tell good stories. The illustrations, too, are splendid.

Do not hesitate to invest, if you see them lying around, in a small book by H. W. L. Moedebeck called *Pocketbook of*

7

Aeronautics published in translation here in 1907 and in the great F. W. Lanchester's *Aerodynamics* (1907) and *Aerodonetics* (1908) which formed the basis of modern aerodynamics.

No one is more aeronautically blessed than he who has the early 'Janes'. Fred T. Jane first issued his *All the World's Airships* in 1909, to be a companion to his famous *All the World's Fighting Ships*. The word 'Airships' which casually covered everything that flew, was changed soon (in 1910) to 'Aircraft', and Jane's *All the World's Aircraft* has unfailingly appeared ever since—with two gaps—as one of the annual air bibles of the world.

Another exhortation to collectors: always buy any books or pamphlets on flying in English published before 1919, and never despise those with apparently childish titles. One of the best air books ever published in the early days was Colonel Harry Delacombe's *The Boy's Book of Airships and other Aerial Craft* (1910) and the author is still with us, hale and hearty to this day. All the books by Grahame-White and Harper—also both happily surviving—are worth having; and look out especially for R. Ferris's *How to Fly*, published in 1910.

The first World War did not produce a great number of books which can be read with enthusiasm today, apart from one or two good histories, notably *The War in the Air* by Jones and Raleigh. But *War Birds* (1927) by an unknown aviator is still an outstanding book—by any standard—of genuine reminiscence, and is most grippingly told.

The between-war period (1918–1939) saw, of course, a veritable flood of air books, including memoirs, and both technical and popular explanations for young and old. The latter, naturally, became obsolete very quickly, and every generation has to re-write such books in the light of the furiously expanding knowledge of the day.

The history of aeronautics came in for an excellent work by E. C. Vivian and W. Lockwood Marsh (*A History of Aeronautics*, 1921) to be followed in 1932 by the greatest history of all time, but in French—C. Dollfus and H. Bouché's *Histoire de l'Aéronautique*. While on this subject one ought to say that English readers only received their first full account of the Wrights in 1944 when the English edition of F. C. Kelly's *The Wright Brothers* appeared. It is a great pity that the same author's edition of the Wright's letters—a truly fascinating volume—has not appeared here. It was published in 1951 in New York, with the title *Miracle at Kitty Hawk: the letters of Wilbur and Orville Wright*.

But an all-embracing American work has now been imported into England, *The Papers of Wilbur and Orville Wright* (2 vols., 1953) a monumental compilation to celebrate the fiftieth anniversary of the world's first powered, controlled and sustained flights in 1903.

The second World War, and the jet age that has followed it, have produced such a spate of books on flying that even to list the highlights would take pages. So perhaps it might be of some help to state one's own ideas about how to go about reading of the air and its ways.

For the general history of Man's efforts to fly, from Greek mythology to the present day, I have to be immodest and recommend my own *A History of Flying* since it is now the only modern all-round history in print with sufficient illustrations (160 of them) to allow the reader to range over the many centuries of thought and the century-and-three-quarters of achievement.

After forming the events of history into some sort of perspective—which I hope I shall have done for the reader—it depends upon which direction his interests take. If you are after what one might call the poetry of flight, read any of Saint-Exupéry's wonderful books in their translations, starting with *Night Flight*. Or you should try Philip Wills's *On Being a Bird* which is an inspired account of gliding, by one of its greatest exponents. On the way, find and keep the little anthology of prose and verse called *Wings*, edited by H. G. Bryden.

Near to poetry is adventure, so try an anthology, *Flying Omnibus*, edited by Paul Jensen; or go to the source books of adventure, written by the men themselves, not only Saint-Exupéry, but Charles Lindbergh (*The Spirit of St. Louis*), Richard Hillary (*The Last Enemy*), Pierre Clostermann (two or three books), and others. Modern pioneering, itself an adventure, is well represented by such great men as Frank Whittle (*Jet: the story of a pioneer*) or Cody (*Pioneer of the Air*, by G. A. Broomfield) apart from the books on the greatest of them all—the Wrights—already mentioned.

A little more technical for the general reader, young or old, are the two *Wonder Books*, one of them entirely on the R.A.F., where he can browse in text and illustrations; or John Taylor's excellent *Picture History of Flight*.

Even more technical, but very well written and illustrated, are James Hay Stevens's *How and Why of Aircraft*, and his *The Shape of the Aeroplane*, an admirable history of the development and evolution of aircraft from the beginning of the century to the present day. D. M. Desoutter's *All About Aircraft* is another excellent general introduction to modern aviation—in many ways, the best of all.

Compilations of aircraft photographs and silhouettes and facts about them are now popular, and the most comprehensive is *The Aircraft of the World* by W. Green and G. Pollinger, which is almost a miniature *Jane*, and is kept up to date in revised editions.

There is at present a dearth—authors and publishers please note—of really good, lucid and intelligently illustrated, books on the theory of flight and general aerodynamics, and the arrival of such books would do much to foster air-mindedness amongst those who are not particularly interested in history or traditions and who are not professionals.

To conclude, we must turn our faces towards the stars. Space travel is in the air, and—whether our readers like it or not—space travel is bound to come within a generation, or two generations at most. I cannot single out individual books of space travel and space fiction (including flying saucers), but it is quite wise to start with those works written by members of the British Interplanetary Society who know what they are talking about, and do not pull your leg with stories about meeting little rubbery men from Mars and chatting to them by telepathy. But there is one 'must' which should be read from cover to cover before you start on a diet of space books. It is the standard—and absorbing—history of rockets and ideas about space travel up to date, by W. Ley, and called *Rockets, Missiles, and Space Travel*.

The literature of flying is now extensive and rewarding, and it is to be hoped that those who are historically minded will adventure more into the past, present and future; and that those who are more technically inclined will find interest and pleasure in following the evolution, first of ideas and then of the vehicles themselves, which have been invented to navigate what Sir George Cayley called 'that uninterrupted navigable ocean that comes to the threshold of every man's door.'

CHARLES H. GIBBS-SMITH.

READING LIST

All publishers are London firms except where otherwise stated. So far as possible dates of the latest editions are given. Prices (net and subject to alteration) are those prevailing in February 1957 and are given only where a book is known to be available new as this list goes to press.

The compiler wishes to thank Mr. F. H. Smith and Mr. G. K. Scott for their kindness in making many valuable suggestions.

I. GENERAL HISTORIES OF FLYING

DOLLFUS, C. and BOUCHÉ, H. *Histoire de l'Aéronautique*. Rev. edn. Paris, *L'Illustration*, 1942.

The most authoritative and most sumptuous general and universal history of flying ever published; with over 2000 illustrations. First published in 1932.

VIVIAN, E. C. and MARSH, W. LOCKWOOD. *A History of Aeronautics*. Collins, 1919.

One of the few and very good general histories from the standpoint of nearly fifty years ago, but crippled for the general reader by its meagre illustrations.

MAGOUN, F. A. and HODGINS, E. *A History of Aircraft*. New York, McGraw-Hill. 1931.

An excellent history of both lighter and heavier than air flying from the beginnings to 1930; well illustrated.

DAVY, M. J. B. *Interpretive History of Flight*. H.M.S.O. 2nd edn. 1948. 8s. 6d.

Another first class history of flying, both heavier and lighter than air, by the former Keeper of Aeronautics at the Science Museum: not very fully illustrated.

GIBBS-SMITH, C. H. *A History of Flying*. Batsford, 1953. 28s.

A history of lighter and heavier than air flying for the general reader from the early myths to 1920, with briefer sections on modern aeronautics: over 150 illustrations.

'YEAR'. *A Pictorial History of Aviation: The complete story of man's conquest of the air from his earliest dreams to the present jet age.* By the editors of *Year.* Los Angeles and New York, 1953.

An ambitious attempt, in over 1000 illustrations, to tell the whole story of flying (including lighter than air, despite the title). Good but naturally biased in favour of later American achievements.

LECORNU, J. *La Navigation Aérienne: Histoire Documentaire et Anecdotique.* 6th edn. Paris, 1913.

A general history of flying to 1913, particularly valuable for its more than 350 illustrations.

MOEDEBECK, H. W. L. *Pocket-Book of Aeronautics.* Translated from the German. Whittaker, 1907.

A curious but useful little book, giving a summary of all aeronautical knowledge of the day, including excellent historical notes on airships, military ballooning and heavier than air experiments, including gliding.

GRAND-CARTERET, J. and DELTEIL, L. *La Conquête de l'Air vue par l'Image (1495–1909).* Paris, 1910.

One of the great collections of early aeronautical illustrations (1495–1909); but infuriating to use as there is no order, chronological or otherwise, to the more than 450 illustrations, owing to its original issue in pot-pourri parts.

HODGSON, J. E. *The History of Aeronautics in Great Britain from the earliest times to the latter half of the Nineteenth Century.* O.U.P., 1924. (Edition limited to 1000 copies).

A modern historical classic. Indispensable, particularly for its detailed coverage of myths and legends in Europe, of the early days of European ballooning and of British ballooning in particular. Very well illustrated and includes an excellent bibliography. Fairly easily obtainable secondhand.

MILBANK, J. *The First Century of Flight in America.* O.U.P. for Princeton U.P. (U.S.A.), 1943.

The only full-length account of early American aeronautics before the Wrights, especially valuable for U.S. ballooning.

13

Supf, P. *Das Buch der deutschen Fluggeschichte.* 2 vols. Berlin. 1935. (Obtainable in England through W. E. Hersant Ltd.)

The standard lavishly illustrated history of German aeronautics. A new edition is in process of issue.

Boffito, G. *Il Volo in Italia.* Florence, 1921.

The standard history of Italian aeronautics; well illustrated.

II. FLIGHTS OF FANCY

Hodgson, J. E. *The History of Aeronautics in Great Britain, etc.* 1924. See note in Section I.

Laufer, B. *The Prehistory of Aviation.* Chicago (Field Museum), 1928.

The only book to give a comprehensive account of ancient Chinese, Indian, Arabian and Classical stories of flight: also, and oddly enough, the best historical account of carrier pigeons.

Nicolson, M. H. *Voyages to the Moon.* Macmillan of New York, 1948. 28*s.*

The delightful history of aerial fantasies from the Middle Ages to Jules Verne, with an invaluable bibliography.

Evans, I. O. *Jules Verne, Master of Science Fiction.* Sidgwick & Jackson, 1956. 12*s.* 6*d.*

An account of the man who made many accurate prophecies and helped to create air-mindedness ahead of his time.

III. LIGHTER-THAN-AIR FLYING

A. General Histories

Tissandier, G. *Histoire des Ballons et des Aéronautes Célèbres, 1783–1890.* 2 vols. Paris, 1887–90.

One of the fine illustrated French histories, told by a distinguished balloonist.

Lecornu, J. *La Navigation Aérienne.* Paris, 1913. See note in Section 1.

BRUEL, F.-L. *Histoire Aeronautique par les Monuments . . . des Origines á 1830.* Paris, 1909 (Supplement 1922).

An 'illustrational' classic, despite the deplorable quality of many of the plates. The supplement is not often found with the main book and is not important.

GRAND-CARTERET, J. and DELTEIL, L. *La Conquête de l'Air, etc.* Paris, 1910. See note in Section I.

VIVIAN, E. C. and MARSH, W. LOCKWOOD. *A History of Aeronautics.* Collins, 1919. See note in Section I.

MARSH, W. LOCKWOOD. *Aeronautical Prints and Drawings.* Halton & Truscott Smith, 1924.

Authoritative text and fine reproductions of the most important early ballooning illustrations, plus a few heavier than air. A 'must' for collectors.

HODGSON, J. E. *The History of Aeronautics in Great Britain, etc.* 1924. See note in Section I.

MAGOUN, F. A. and HODGINS, E. *A History of Aircraft.* 1931. See note in Section I.

DOLLFUS, C. and BOUCHÉ, H. *Histoire de l'Aéronautique.* 1942. See note in Section I.

DAVY, M. J. B. *Interpretive History of Flight.* 2nd edn. 1948. See note in Section I.

GIBBS-SMITH, C. H. *A History of Flying.* 1953. See note in Section I.

B. Special Studies

LANA, F. *The Aerial Ship 1670.* (No. 4 of the Aeronautical Classics republished by the Royal Aeronautical Society, 1910.)

The ingenious and first rational, although unworkable, design for a balloon in history; with prophetic accounts of air warfare.

LA VAULX, Comte de, and TISSANDIER, P. *Joseph et Étienne Montgolfier.* Annonay, 1926.

The major work on the inventors of the hot-air balloon.

15

LUNARDI, V. *Account of the First Aerial Voyage in England.* 1784.

A rare classic in which the Tuscan secretary of the Neapolitan ambassador in London recounts his famous flight.

CAVALLO, T. *The History and Practice of Aerostation.* 1785.

A very rare classic and the first full-dress technical manual on ballooning to be published in English. Also valuable for its accounts of the first flights.

MASON, T. MONCK. *Aeronautica: or Sketches Illustrative of the Theory and Practice of Aerostation, etc.* 1838.

The story, by one of the aeronauts who took part, of the famous balloon voyage from London to Weilburg in 1836; also valuable for accounts of other early aeronauts.

TURNOR, C. HATTON. *Astra Castra: Experiments and Adventures in the atmosphere.* 1865.

A great pot-pourri of legend and truth about flying, up to the mid-century. A collector's 'must'.

MARION, F. *Wonderful Balloon Ascents, etc.* (Library of Wonders) Cassell. 1870.

A popular Victorian book of ballooning history, translated from *Les Ballons et les Voyages Aériens*, 1867.

GLAISHER, J. (and others). *Travels in the Air.* Rev. edn. 1871.

A number of famous flights recounted, including Glaisher's famous ascents of 1862. Translated from *Voyages Aériens*, 1870.

FONVIELLE, W. DE. *Adventures in the Air.* Translated from the French by J. S. Keltie. 1877.

Another popular recital of famous ballooning events. Translated from *Aventures Aériennes, etc.* 1874.

COXWELL, H. *My Life and Balloon Experiences.* 2 vols. W. H. Allen, 1887–89.

One of the classic aerial autobiographies by perhaps the greatest Victorian balloonist.

MOEDEBECK, H. W. L. *Pocket-Book of Aeronautics.* 1907. See note in Section I.

HILDEBRANDT, A. *Airships Past and Present*. Trans. from the German. Constable, 1908.

The history and practice of ballooning, with chapters on airships and early aviation. The word 'airship' at that time covered all aircraft.

DELACOMBE, H. *The Boy's Book of Airships and other Aerial Craft*. Richards, 1910.

A good account of contemporary balloon and aeroplane flying.

ANDRÉE, S. A. *The Andrée Diaries*. Lane, 1931. Trans. from the Official Swedish edn. by E. Adams-Ray.

The astonishing story, with all the documents, of the Andrée balloon attempt to cross the North Pole in 1897, and the discovery of the bodies, diaries, photographs, etc., of the expedition in 1930.

WILKINSON, S. *Lighter than Air*. Stockwell, 1939.

Reminiscences of a modern balloon pilot.

MILBANK, J. *The First Century of Flight in America*. 1943. See note in Section I.

BREWER, G. *Fifty Years of Flying*. 1946. See note in Section IV C.

GIBBS-SMITH, C. H. *Ballooning*. Penguin (King Penguin), 1948.

Thirty-two plates and short descriptions of the highlights of ballooning history.

C. Dirigibles

SANTOS-DUMONT, A. *My Airships: the story of my Life*. Richards, 1904.

A minor classic. The autobiography of the man who made Europe air-minded with his small airships, 1898–1904; and later (1906) made the first official powered flight in Europe.

WHALE, G. *British Airships, Past, Present and Future*. Lane, 1920.

A standard history of British dirigibles.

SPRIGG, C. ST. J. *The Airship, its Design, History, Operation and Future*. Sampson Low, 1931.

A general survey.

17

SINCLAIR, J. A. *Airships in Peace and War*. Rich & Cowan, 1934.
A general survey.

LEHMANN, E. A. and ADELT, L. *Zeppelin*. Longmans, 1937. Trans. by Jay Dratler.

The story of the Zeppelins told by one of their great commanders, who perished in the *Hindenburg* disaster.

NIELSEN, T. *The Zeppelin Story*. Wingate, 1955. 17s. 6d.

The history of the most successful type of dirigible ever invented, and of its great men, especially Dr. Eckener.

IV. HEAVIER-THAN-AIR FLYING

A. General Histories

JANE, F. T. *All the World's Airships*. Sampson Low, 1909.

—— *All the World's Aircraft* Sampson Low, 1910 (and then annually—except 1915 and 1921—to date).

Classics and indispensables. Photographs and specifications of almost everything that has flown since 1903. The word 'airships' meant aircraft in general at the time. Early volumes also contain names of all qualified British pilots.

GRAND-CARTERET, J. and DELTEIL, L. *La Conquête de l'Air, etc.* Paris, 1910. See note in Section I.

VIVIAN, E. C. and MARSH, W. LOCKWOOD (etc.). *A History of Aeronautics*. 1919. See note in Section I.

MAGOUN, F. A. and HODGINS, E. *A History of Aircraft*. 1931. See note in Section I.

DOLLFUS, C. and BOUCHÉ, H. (etc.). *Histoire de l'Aéronautique*. 1942. See note in Section I.

DAVY, M. J. B. *Interpretive History of Flight*. 1948. See note in Section I.

DORMAN, G. *Fifty Years Fly-past: from Wright Brothers to Comet*. Forbes-Robertson, 1951. 15s.

A general history since 1903.

18

STEVENS, J. H. *The Shape of the Aeroplane.* Hutchinson, 1953. 12s. 6d.

The only book to trace the technical development of aircraft structure and function from the Wrights to the 1950's.

'YEAR'. *A Pictorial History of Aviation, etc.* 1953. See note in Section 1.

GIBBS-SMITH, C. H. *A History of Flying.* 1953. See note in Section I.

ROLFE, D. and DAWYDOFF, A. *Airplanes of the World, from Pusher to Jet,* 1490 to 1954. New York, Simon & Schuster, 1954.

A collection of over 800 drawings (with rather inadequate information) of aircraft from the earliest times to the 1950's.

TAYLOR, J. W. R. *A Picture History of Flight.* Hulton, 1955. 25s.

Admirable pictorial history—mostly aviation and mostly British —from 1900, with over 600 photographs, etc.

GREEN, W. and CROSS, R. *The Jet Aircraft of the World.* Macdonald, 1955. 30s.

Illustrates and describes all the important jet aircraft from the first—the He 176 of 1939—to date.

SMITH, G. G. *Gas Turbines and Jet Propulsion.* 6th edn. rev. by F. C. Sheffield. Iliffe, 1955. 35s.

Includes a short history of jet propulsion.

GIBBS-SMITH, C. H. *A Short History of the Aeroplane.* (Science Museum handbook) H.M.S.O. 1957. (forthcoming).

The story of heavier-than-air flight from classical legend until the present day. Includes some 150 illustrations.

B. Before the Wrights

CHANUTE, O. *Progress in Flying Machines.* New York, American Engineer. 1894.

A classic, a rarity and an 'indispensable'. The entire field of suggestions and achievements (gliders and models) in aviation scientifically surveyed by one of the great men of aeronautics.

19

DOLLFUS, C. and BOUCHÉ, H. (etc.). *Histoire de l'Aéronautique.* 1942. See note in Section I.

BREWER, G. and ALEXANDER, P. Y. *Aeronautics: an Abridgement of Aeronautical Specifications filed in the Patent Office.* 1815–91. 1893.

A rarity of specialised interest; but it makes amusing and often fantastic reading.

LECORNU, J. *La Navigation Aérienne.* Paris, 1913. See note in Section I.

MOEDEBECK, H. W. L. *Pocket-Book of Aeronautics.* 1907. See note in Section I.

UCCELLI, A. *I Libri del Volo di Leonardo da Vinci:* Milan (Hoepli), 1952.

A complete survey of Leonardo's work in aeronautics, including some 400 facsimiles of his drawings.

PRITCHARD, J. L. *Sir George Cayley, Bart., the Father of British Aeronautics: the Man and his Work.* J. Roy. Aeron. Soc., February, 1955. 10*s.*

The only comprehensive work, excellent and indispensable, on the true father of the modern aeroplane, who was a great man and a great inventor.

CAYLEY, Sir G. *On Aerial Navigation,* 1809–10. (Reprinted as No. 1 of the Aeronautical Classics Series, 1910).

Cayley's original magazine articles, which laid the foundations of mechanical flight.

CAYLEY, Sir G. *Aeronautical and Miscellaneous Note-Book* (c. 1799–1826) of Sir George Cayley, with . . . a list of the Cayley papers. Edited, with introduction, by J. E. Hodgson, Cambridge (Newcomen Society), 1933.

Cayley's famous note-book, edited by the man who virtually re-discovered and established him in history.

DAVY, M. J. B. *Henson and Stringfellow, their work in Aeronautics.* (Science Museum handbook). H.M.S.O. 1931.

A pioneer book whose conclusions on Stringfellow have now

been drastically altered by Ballantyne and Pritchard (see below).

BALLANTYNE, A. M. and PRITCHARD, J. L. *The Lives and Work of William Samuel Henson and John Stringfellow. J. Roy. Aeron. Soc.* June, 1956. 10s.

The work which has decisively overturned the claim that Stringfellow made the first successful powered model aeroplane. A 'must' for aero-historians.

WENHAM, F. H. *Aerial Locomotion*, 1866. No. 2 of the Aeronautical Classics republished by the Aeronautical (later Royal) Society, 1910.

A classic paper on aviation read at the first meeting of the Aeronautical (later Royal) Society in 1866.

MAREY, E. J. *Animal Mechanism: a Treatise on Terrestrial and Aerial Locomotion.* Trans. from the French. 1874.

One of the pioneer investigations of bird flight, which was read by all the early aviation pioneers and stimulated much subsequent work. Tr. from *La Machine Animale*, 1873.

HALLE, G. *Otto Lilienthal.* 2nd edn. Düsseldorf,1956.

The only biography of one of the aviation giants. Will probably be published in English soon.

LILIENTHAL, O. *Bird Flight as a Basis of Aviation.* Longmans, 1911.

One of the classics by one of the giants of flying. He first published this (in German) in 1889, before making his epoch-making gliding flights of 1891–96.

PILCHER, P. *Gliding*, 1890. No. 5 of the Aeronautical Classics, republished by the Royal Aeronautical Society, 1910. 10s.

The personal narrative of England's great gliding pioneer who was killed in 1899, and who, if he had lived, might well have antedated the Wrights in powered flight.

LANGLEY, S. M. *Langley Memoir of Mechanical Flight.* 2 parts (part 2 by C. M. Manly). Washington, D.C. (Smithsonian Institution), 1911.

A great man's own account of his researches and ultimate failure in 1903 to achieve powered flight. A classic.

C. The Early Years of Practical Flying

KELLY, F. C. *The Wright Brothers*. Harrap, 1944.

The only full-length story of the Wrights, written by a life-long friend. Not very useful from the technical standpoint.

WRIGHT, W. & O. *The Papers of Wilbur and Orville Wright*. 2 vols. McGraw-Hill, New York, 1953. £9. 7s. 6d.

The monumental edition of the letters and papers of the Wrights; profusely illustrated and accompanied by an explanatory commentary, detailed appendices, etc.

PRITCHARD, J. L. *The Wright Brothers and the Royal Aeronautical Society. J. Roy. Aeron. Soc.*, December, 1953. 10s.

Includes expert general assessments of the work of the Wrights, etc.

GIBBS-SMITH, C. H. *A Short History of the Aeroplane*. H.M.S.O., 1957. See note in Section IV A. Includes an account of the main influences forming the first decade of practical aviation.

FERRIS, R. *How to Fly; or the Conquest of the Air*. Nelson, 1910.

A mine of detailed information, both textual and illustrational, of contemporary aeroplanes. A key work.

DELACOMBE, H. *The Boy's Book of Airships and other Aerial Craft*. Richards, 1910.

An excellent account of contemporary balloon and aeroplane flying.

GRAHAME-WHITE, C., and HARPER, H. *The Aeroplane, Past, Present and Future*. T. Werner Laurie. 1911.

A 'must' for those interested in the first generation of practical aeroplanes.

BRETT, R. D. *The History of British Aviation, 1908–14*. John Hamilton, 1934.

A very detailed chronological account of the 'early days'. Later issued in 2 vols.

LANCHESTER, F. W. *Aerodynamics*. Constable, 1907.

—— *Aerodonetics*. Constable, 1908.

The two classic books which, although spurned at the time, laid the foundations of modern aerodynamic theory.

BARBER, H. *The Aeroplane Speaks*. 7th edn. McBride, Nast. 1918.

An instructional manual of little interest as such today; but valuable for its more than 240 illustrations of European and other aircraft types from 1903 to 1918.

TURNER, C. C. *The Old Flying Days*. Sampson Low, 1927.

A pioneer's reminiscences of flying, both in balloons and aeroplanes.

HARPER, H. *Twenty-five Years of Flying*. Hutchinson, 1929.

Reminiscences of a pioneer aviation journalist.

BREWER, G. *Fifty Years of Flying*. Rolls House, 1946.

Reminiscences of ballooning and aviation by one of the great figures of British aeronautics, who was also the Wright's patent agent here.

BROOMFIELD, G. A. *Pioneer of the Air*. [*S. F. Cody*.] Gale & Polden, 1953. 10s. 6d.

One of the grand old men of British Aviation (naturalised from America) who made the first official aeroplane flight here in 1908.

D. Modern Flying

HUNSAKER, J. C. *Aeronautics at the Mid-Century*. O.U.P. for Yale U.P., 1952. 24s.

A general survey by an American authority.

TAYLOR, J. W. R. *The Eagle Book of Aircraft*. Hulton Press, 1953. 10s. 6d.

'FLIGHT'. *Flight Handbook: the Theory and Practice of Aeronautics*. 5th edn. Iliffe, 1954. 15s.

An introduction to modern aeronautics: fully illustrated.

DESOUTTER, D. M. *All About Aircraft*. Faber, 1954. 25s.

An admirable general description of the multiple facets of modern aviation; the how, the what and the why: fully illustrated.

GREEN, W. and POLLINGER, G. *The Aircraft of the World*. Rev. edn. Macdonald, 1956. 35s.

Illustrations and descriptions of virtually every aircraft flying

23

today. Over 1000 photographs and some hundreds of silhouettes. A 'must' for anyone interested in modern aircraft.

GIBBS-SMITH, C. H. and BRADFORD, L. E. *World Aircraft Recognition Manual*. Putnam, 1956. 15*s*.

Photographs, and in many cases silhouettes, of over 240 aircraft with brief descriptions.

Wonder Book of Aircraft. Ward Lock, 1956. 15*s*.

WALLACE, G. *The Flight of Alcock and Brown*. Putnam, 1955. 18*s*.

The fullest account of the first direct transatlantic flight in history (1919).

LINDBERGH, C. A. *The Spirit of St. Louis*. Murray, 1953. 25*s*.

Lindbergh's own account of his historic solo flight—the first *solo* but not the first *flight*—across the North Atlantic in 1927.

SAINT-EXUPÉRY, A. DE. *Night Flight*. Appleton, U.S.A., 1935; Heinemann. Penguin, 1939.

—— *Wind, Sand and Stars*. Heinemann, 1939. 10*s*. 6*d*.
See Introduction.

COBHAM, Sir A. J. *Skyways*. Nisbet, 1925.

VERDON-ROE, Sir A. *The World of Wings and Things*. Hurst & Blackett, 1939.

WHITTLE, Sir F. *Jet*. Muller, 1954. 18*s*.

HEINKEL, E. *He. 1000*. Hutchinson, 1956. 30*s*.

BRABAZON OF TARA, Lord. *The Brabazon Story*. Heinemann, 1956. 25*s*.

Five famous autobiographies whose authors' names speak for themselves.

JENSEN, PAUL, ed. *Flying Omnibus*. Cassell, 1953. 7*s*. 6*d*.
See Introduction.

E. Miscellaneous Aircraft

GREGORY, H. F. *The Helicopter*. Allen & Unwin, 1948.

The only comprehensive history of the modern helicopter.

SHAPIRO, JACOB. *The Helicopter*. Muller, 1957. 21*s*.

A non-technical description of the design and capabilities of helicopters.

LECORNU, J. *Les Cerfs Volants*. Paris, 1902.

The only considerable work on the history of kite-flying.

WEISS, J. B. *Gliding and Soaring Flight*. Sampson Low, 1923.

A general history and an account of gliding technique.

SITEK, A. and BLUNT, V. *Gliding and Soaring*. Alliance Press, 1944.

A full account of gliding theory and practice.

HORSLEY, T. *Soaring Flight: the Art of Gliding*. Eyre & Spottis-woode, 1944.

A fine general work.

WILLS, P. A. *On Being a Bird*. Parrish, 1953. 15*s*. 6*d*.

One of the best and most poetic books on flying, by one of the finest exponents of gliding.

MURPHY, C. J. *Parachute*. New York, Putnam, 1930.

An account of how the automatic parachute was invented, almost perfected, and then lost sight of before its reinvention at great cost.

DIXON, C. *Parachuting*. S. Low, 1930.

A general account of parachuting.

LOW, A. M. *Parachutes in Peace and War*. Gifford, 1942.

Another general account.

V. WAR IN THE AIR

JONES, H. A. and RALEIGH, Sir W. *The War in the Air*. 6 vols (with appendix). O.U.P., 1922–37, now H.M.S.O. Vols. 1 and 5, o.p. Vols. 2–4 each 21*s*. Vol. 6, with appendix, 30*s*.

The official history of British air warfare in World War I.

BRUCE, J. M. *British Aeroplanes, 1914–18*. Putnam (forthcoming), 1957. 12 *gns*.

Will undoubtedly become a standard work.

SPRINGS, E. W., ed. *War Birds*. Garden City Pubg. Co. new edn. 1938.

A World War I classic.

TEMPLEWOOD, 1st VISCOUNT (S. J. G. Hoare). *Empire of the Air*. Collins, 1957. 21s.

A personal account of the rise of British air power from the politician's point of view.

GREY, C. G. *History of the Air Ministry*. Allen & Unwin, 1940.

A typically outspoken work by the greatest of British aeronautical journalists.

MINISTRY OF INFORMATION. *The Battle of Britain*. H.M.S.O., 1941.

A minor classic; written anonymously by Hilary St. George Saunders.

RICHEY, P. *Fighter Pilot*. Rev. edn. Hutchinson, 1955. 10s. 6d.; paper covered 2s. 6d.

One of the classics of World War II: first published in 1941.

HILLARY, RICHARD. *The Last Enemy*. Macmillan, 1943. 10s.

Reminiscences, factual and spiritual, of a World War II fighter pilot. A classic.

RAWNSLEY, C. F. and WRIGHT, ROBERT. *Night Fighter*. Collins, 1957. 18s.

The vivid record of John Cunningham's brilliant team in World War II.

CHESHIRE, L. *Bomber Pilot*. Hutchinson, 1943. 9s. 6d.; (Arrow Books, paper cover) 2s. 6d.

A World War II classic.

NARRACOTT, A. H. *Air Power in War*. Muller, 1945.

A study by the aeronautical correspondent of *The Times*.

PARTRIDGE, E. *A Dictionary of R.A.F. Slang*. Michael Joseph, 1945.

SAUNDERS, H. ST. G. *Per Ardua: the Rise of British Air Power*, 1911–39. O.U.P., 1945.

A standard history, brilliantly told.

MINISTRY OF INFORMATION. *Merchant Airmen: the Air Ministry Account of British Civil Aviation*, 1939–44. H.M.S.O., 1946.

One of the admirable official accounts of wartime aviation.

RICHARDS, D. and SAUNDERS, H. ST. G. *The Royal Air Force, 1939–1945*. 3 vols. H.M.S.O. 1953–4. 40s. 6d. the set.

The standard, although preliminary, official history.

KEMP, P. K. *Fleet Air Arm*. Jenkins, 1954. 16s.

The story of British Naval flying by the Admiralty archivist.

BRADDON, R. *Cheshire, V.C.* Evans, 1954. 15s.

The story of a remarkable pilot and humanitarian.

BARNHAM, D. *One Man's Window*. Kimber, 1956. 18s.

A remarkable introspective analysis of fear and its conquest by a Spitfire pilot who fought in the defence of Malta.

BABINGTON-SMITH, C. *Evidence in Camera*. Chatto & Windus (forthcoming), 1957.

The history of aerial photographic reconnaissance, particularly in the last war, by a woman who was one of the master photo-interpreters of the R.A.F.

LEE, A. *The German Air Force*. Duckworth, 1946. 21s.

—— *The Soviet Air Force*. New edn. Duckworth, 1952. 10s. 6d.

The most comprehensive accounts of these two Services.

BARTZ, K. *Swastika in the Air*. Kimber, 1956.

A good account, although biased, of the struggle and defeat of the German Air Force, 1939–45.

REITSCH, H. *The Sky My Kingdom*. Bodley Head, 1955.

Reminiscences of the famous German woman pilot who flew a piloted flying-bomb and test flew the Me 163 rocket plane.

GALLAND, A. *The First and the Last*. Methuen, 1955. 21s.

Reminiscences of one of Hitler's crack fighter pilots.

THETFORD, O. G. *Aircraft of the Royal Air Force, 1938–57*. Putnam, 1957. 50s.
27

LEE, A. *Air Power*. Duckworth, 1955. 15*s*.

A study of air power in the modern world.

GREEN, W. and FORREST, I. *The Air Forces of the World*. Macdonald (forthcoming).

Wonder Book of the R.A.F. Ward Lock, New edn. in preparation. 1957. 15*s*.

VI. MISCELLANEOUS

BRYDEN, H. G. ed. *Wings: an Anthology of Flight*. Faber, 1942.

Flying's only anthology of prose and verse.

HUGHES, A. J. *A History of Air Navigation*. Allen & Unwin, 1946. 10*s*. 6*d*.

HURREN, B. J. *Fellowship of the Air*. Iliffe, 1951. 30*s*.

An accurate and entertaining history of the Royal Aero Club.

KARMAN, T. M. *Aerodynamics: Selected Topics in the Light of their Historical Development*. O.U.P. for Princeton U.P., 1954. 38*s*.

An essay by the greatest living aerodynamicist.

PAYNE, L. G. S. *Air Dates*. Heinemann (forthcoming) App. 42*s*.

A 500-page compendium of flying dates, three-quarters of which deal with the years 1939–56, but useful occasionally for earlier times.

PEREIRA, H. B. *Aircraft Badges and Markings*. Adlard Coles, Southampton (dist. Harrap), 1955. 5*s*.

The first book to gather together the new 'heraldry' and markings of aircraft, from early in the century up to date.

PUDNEY, J. *Laboratory of the Air*. H.M.S.O., 1948. 3*s*. 6*d*.

A short history of the Royal Aircraft Establishment at Farnborough.

ROBERTSON, B. *Aircraft Camouflage and Markings, 1907–54*. Harleyford Publications, Marlow, Bucks., 1956. 45*s*.

Mostly service aircraft.

RUPPELT, E. J. *The Report on Unidentified Flying Objects.* Gollancz, 1956. 18s. 6d.

MICHEL, A. *The Truth about Flying Saucers.* Hale, 1957. 15s.

The two best books, amongst the ever increasing number on this intriguing subject.

Rockets and Space Travel

LEY, W. *Rockets, Missiles and Space Travel.* 2nd edn. Chapman & Hall, 1951. 35s.

The standard history of the subject, along with detailed discussions of the problems of space-flight.

GATLAND, K. W. *Development of the Guided Missile.* 2nd edn. Iliffe, 1954. 15s.

A 'must' for anyone interested in rocketry and guided missiles.

DORNBERGER, W. *V2.* Trans. by J. Cleugh and G. Halliday. Hurst & Blackett, 1954. 16s.

The authentic German story of the first successful long range rocket of history.

Air Terms

BECKFORD, L. *An ABC of Aeronautics.* Cassell, 1957. 15s.

BRITISH STANDARDS INSTITUTION. *Glossary of Aeronautical Terms.* 4th edn. 1950–52.

INDEX OF AUTHORS

www.ingramcontent.com/pod-product-compliance
Ingram Content Group UK Ltd.
Pitfield, Milton Keynes, MK11 3LW, UK
UKHW020449010325
455719UK00015B/494

9 781107 622203